MW01247746

50 Breakfast Lover's Cookbook

By: Kelly Johnson

Table of Contents

- Smoked Salmon and Cream Cheese Bagel
- Potato and Cheese Breakfast Skillet
- Overnight Oats with Fruit and Nuts
- Cinnamon Sugar Donuts
- Maple Pecan Pancakes
- Eggs in a Hole with Toast
- Oatmeal with Brown Sugar and Raisins
- Scrambled Eggs with Salsa and Sour Cream
- Ricotta Pancakes with Lemon Zest
- Spinach and Mushroom Frittata
- Breakfast Quesadilla with Sausage
- Sausage Patties with Biscuit Gravy
- Warm Cinnamon Rolls with Cream Cheese Frosting
- Egg and Veggie Breakfast Wrap
- Coconut Banana Smoothie

Classic Pancakes with Maple Syrup

Ingredients

- 1 1/2 cups all-purpose flour
- 3 1/2 tsp baking powder
- 1 tsp salt
- 1 tbsp sugar
- 1 1/4 cups milk
- 1 large egg
- 3 tbsp melted butter
- Maple syrup for serving

Instructions

1. In a large bowl, whisk together flour, baking powder, salt, and sugar.
2. In another bowl, beat together milk, egg, and melted butter.
3. Pour the wet ingredients into the dry ingredients and stir until just combined (lumps are fine).
4. Heat a griddle or skillet over medium heat and lightly grease with butter or oil.
5. Pour 1/4 cup of batter onto the griddle for each pancake. Cook until bubbles form on the surface, then flip and cook until golden brown on both sides.
6. Serve with maple syrup.

Fluffy Buttermilk Waffles

Ingredients

- 2 cups all-purpose flour
- 2 tbsp sugar
- 1 tbsp baking powder
- 1/2 tsp baking soda
- 1/2 tsp salt
- 1 3/4 cups buttermilk
- 1/2 cup unsalted butter, melted
- 2 large eggs
- 1 tsp vanilla extract

Instructions

1. Preheat your waffle iron according to the manufacturer's instructions.
2. In a large bowl, combine flour, sugar, baking powder, baking soda, and salt.
3. In a separate bowl, whisk together buttermilk, melted butter, eggs, and vanilla extract.
4. Pour the wet ingredients into the dry ingredients and stir until just combined.
5. Lightly grease the waffle iron and pour the batter onto it. Close and cook according to the waffle iron's instructions, typically for 3-5 minutes, until golden and crispy.
6. Serve with syrup, whipped cream, or fresh berries.

Eggs Benedict with Hollandaise Sauce

Ingredients

- 4 large eggs
- 2 English muffins, split
- 4 slices Canadian bacon
- 1/2 cup unsalted butter
- 2 egg yolks
- 1 tbsp lemon juice
- Salt and pepper to taste

Instructions

1. To poach the eggs: Bring a pot of water to a simmer. Crack each egg into a small bowl and gently slide into the water. Cook for about 4 minutes, until whites are set but yolks are still runny. Remove with a slotted spoon and set aside.
2. For the hollandaise sauce: Melt butter in a saucepan. In a separate bowl, whisk egg yolks and lemon juice. Slowly drizzle the warm butter into the egg mixture while whisking constantly, until the sauce thickens. Season with salt and pepper.
3. Toast the English muffin halves and briefly fry the Canadian bacon in a skillet.
4. To assemble: Place a slice of Canadian bacon on each muffin half, top with a poached egg, and spoon over the hollandaise sauce. Serve immediately.

Scrambled Eggs with Herbs

Ingredients

- 4 large eggs
- 2 tbsp butter
- Salt and pepper to taste
- 1 tbsp fresh chives, chopped
- 1 tbsp fresh parsley, chopped

Instructions

1. Crack the eggs into a bowl and whisk until well combined.
2. Melt butter in a skillet over medium heat.
3. Pour in the eggs and cook, stirring gently, for 2-3 minutes until soft curds form.
4. Season with salt and pepper, and stir in fresh herbs.
5. Serve warm with toast or your favorite breakfast sides.

Avocado Toast with Poached Egg

Ingredients

- 2 slices of your favorite bread
- 1 ripe avocado
- 2 large eggs
- Salt and pepper to taste
- Red pepper flakes (optional)
- Lemon juice (optional)

Instructions

1. Toast the slices of bread until golden and crisp.
2. Mash the avocado in a bowl and season with salt, pepper, and a squeeze of lemon juice if desired.
3. Poach the eggs in simmering water for about 4 minutes, until the whites are set but the yolks remain runny.
4. Spread mashed avocado evenly on the toast and top each slice with a poached egg.
5. Sprinkle with red pepper flakes and extra seasoning if desired. Serve immediately.

Cinnamon Roll Pancakes

Ingredients

- 1 1/2 cups all-purpose flour
- 1 tbsp sugar
- 1 tbsp baking powder
- 1/2 tsp salt
- 1 cup milk
- 1 large egg
- 2 tbsp butter, melted
- 1/2 tsp vanilla extract
- 1/4 cup brown sugar
- 1 tsp ground cinnamon
- Cream cheese icing for topping

Instructions

1. In a bowl, whisk together flour, sugar, baking powder, and salt.
2. In another bowl, combine milk, egg, butter, and vanilla extract. Add the wet ingredients to the dry ingredients and stir until just combined.
3. In a small bowl, mix together brown sugar and cinnamon.
4. Heat a griddle over medium heat and lightly grease. Pour 1/4 cup batter onto the griddle. Sprinkle with cinnamon sugar, then pour a little more batter over the top. Cook until bubbles form on the surface, then flip and cook until golden brown.
5. Drizzle with cream cheese icing before serving.

French Toast with Fresh Berries

Ingredients

- 4 slices of bread (preferably day-old)
- 2 large eggs
- 1/2 cup milk
- 1 tsp vanilla extract
- 1/4 tsp ground cinnamon
- Butter for frying
- Fresh berries (strawberries, blueberries, raspberries)
- Maple syrup for serving

Instructions

1. In a shallow bowl, whisk together eggs, milk, vanilla extract, and cinnamon.
2. Heat butter in a skillet over medium heat.
3. Dip each slice of bread into the egg mixture, coating both sides, then fry in the skillet for 2-3 minutes per side until golden brown.
4. Serve the French toast topped with fresh berries and a drizzle of maple syrup.

Sausage and Egg Breakfast Casserole

Ingredients

- 1 lb breakfast sausage
- 1/2 cup onion, chopped
- 1 cup shredded cheddar cheese
- 6 large eggs
- 1 cup milk
- 1/2 tsp salt
- 1/2 tsp black pepper
- 1/2 tsp garlic powder
- 6 slices of bread, cubed

Instructions

1. Preheat the oven to 350°F (175°C).
2. Cook the sausage in a skillet over medium heat, breaking it up with a spoon until browned. Add onion and cook for another 2-3 minutes.
3. In a bowl, whisk together eggs, milk, salt, pepper, and garlic powder.
4. Grease a 9x13-inch baking dish and layer the cubed bread at the bottom. Top with sausage mixture and shredded cheese.
5. Pour the egg mixture over the top and bake for 30-35 minutes, until set and golden.
6. Let cool slightly before serving.

Veggie Omelette with Feta

Ingredients

- 3 large eggs
- 1/4 cup milk
- 1/4 cup red bell pepper, diced
- 1/4 cup spinach, chopped
- 1/4 cup onion, chopped
- 1/4 cup feta cheese, crumbled
- Salt and pepper to taste
- Olive oil for cooking

Instructions

1. Whisk together the eggs and milk in a bowl. Season with salt and pepper.
2. Heat a small amount of olive oil in a skillet over medium heat. Add the diced bell pepper, onion, and spinach. Cook for 2-3 minutes until softened.
3. Pour the egg mixture over the veggies and cook for 2-3 minutes until the edges begin to set. Sprinkle with feta cheese.
4. Carefully flip the omelette and cook for an additional 1-2 minutes until fully set.
5. Serve warm.

Breakfast Burrito with Bacon and Avocado

Ingredients

- 2 large eggs
- 2 slices bacon, cooked
- 1/4 avocado, sliced
- 1 large flour tortilla
- 1/4 cup shredded cheddar cheese
- 2 tbsp salsa
- Salt and pepper to taste

Instructions

1. Scramble the eggs in a skillet over medium heat until fully cooked. Season with salt and pepper.
2. Lay the tortilla flat and sprinkle with shredded cheese. Add the scrambled eggs, cooked bacon, avocado slices, and salsa.
3. Roll up the tortilla tightly into a burrito, folding in the edges as you go.
4. Serve immediately.

Sweet Potato Hash with Eggs

Ingredients

- 1 large sweet potato, peeled and diced
- 1 tbsp olive oil
- 1/4 cup onion, chopped
- 1/4 cup bell pepper, chopped
- 1 tsp paprika
- Salt and pepper to taste
- 2 large eggs

Instructions

1. Heat olive oil in a large skillet over medium heat. Add the diced sweet potato and cook for 5-7 minutes until tender.
2. Add the chopped onion and bell pepper and cook for another 2-3 minutes. Season with paprika, salt, and pepper.
3. In a separate skillet, cook the eggs to your preference (fried, scrambled, or poached).
4. Serve the sweet potato hash topped with the cooked eggs.

Breakfast Quiche with Spinach and Cheese

Ingredients

- 1 pre-made pie crust
- 1 cup spinach, chopped
- 1/2 cup shredded mozzarella cheese
- 1/2 cup shredded cheddar cheese
- 3 large eggs
- 1 cup heavy cream
- Salt and pepper to taste

Instructions

1. Preheat the oven to 375°F (190°C).
2. In a skillet, cook the spinach over medium heat until wilted.
3. In a bowl, whisk together the eggs, heavy cream, salt, and pepper.
4. Place the cooked spinach in the pie crust and top with mozzarella and cheddar cheese. Pour the egg mixture over the top.
5. Bake for 30-35 minutes, or until the quiche is set and golden. Let cool slightly before slicing.

Croissant Breakfast Sandwich with Ham and Cheese

Ingredients

- 1 croissant, split
- 1 egg
- 2 slices ham
- 1 slice Swiss cheese
- Salt and pepper to taste

Instructions

1. In a skillet, cook the egg to your preference (fried, scrambled, or poached).
2. Toast the croissant halves in the skillet or oven.
3. Layer the bottom half of the croissant with the cooked egg, ham slices, and Swiss cheese.
4. Top with the other half of the croissant and serve warm.

Banana Bread French Toast

Ingredients

- 2 slices banana bread
- 2 large eggs
- 1/2 cup milk
- 1 tsp vanilla extract
- 1/2 tsp cinnamon
- Butter for cooking
- Maple syrup for serving

Instructions

1. In a bowl, whisk together eggs, milk, vanilla, and cinnamon.
2. Heat butter in a skillet over medium heat.
3. Dip the slices of banana bread into the egg mixture, coating both sides. Cook in the skillet for 2-3 minutes per side until golden brown.
4. Serve with a drizzle of maple syrup.

Smoothie Bowls with Granola and Fruit

Ingredients

- 1 frozen banana
- 1/2 cup frozen berries
- 1/4 cup almond milk (or any milk of choice)
- 1 tbsp honey
- 1/4 cup granola
- Fresh fruit (berries, banana slices, etc.)

Instructions

1. In a blender, combine the frozen banana, frozen berries, almond milk, and honey. Blend until smooth.
2. Pour the smoothie into a bowl.
3. Top with granola and fresh fruit. Serve immediately.

Chia Pudding with Almond Butter and Berries

Ingredients

- 1/2 cup chia seeds
- 1 cup almond milk
- 1 tbsp honey or maple syrup
- 1/4 cup almond butter
- Fresh berries for topping

Instructions

1. In a bowl, mix chia seeds, almond milk, and honey. Stir well, then cover and refrigerate for at least 2 hours or overnight to thicken.
2. Once the chia pudding is set, stir in almond butter and top with fresh berries.
3. Serve chilled.

Banana Oatmeal with Honey and Walnuts

Ingredients

- 1 cup rolled oats
- 2 cups water or milk
- 1 ripe banana, mashed
- 1 tbsp honey
- 1/4 cup walnuts, chopped
- Pinch of cinnamon (optional)

Instructions

1. In a saucepan, bring water or milk to a simmer.
2. Add the oats and cook according to package instructions.
3. Stir in the mashed banana, honey, and cinnamon (if using).
4. Cook for an additional 2-3 minutes, allowing the banana to soften and sweeten the oats.
5. Top with chopped walnuts and serve warm.

Huevos Rancheros

Ingredients

- 2 corn tortillas
- 2 large eggs
- 1/2 cup salsa
- 1/4 cup crumbled queso fresco
- 1/4 cup sour cream
- Fresh cilantro for garnish
- Salt and pepper to taste

Instructions

1. Heat the tortillas in a dry skillet until lightly browned and crispy.
2. In the same skillet, cook the eggs sunny-side up or to your preferred doneness.
3. Top each tortilla with an egg, then spoon salsa over the eggs.
4. Garnish with queso fresco, sour cream, and fresh cilantro.
5. Serve immediately with a side of beans or avocado if desired.

Breakfast Tacos with Chorizo

Ingredients

- 2 small flour tortillas
- 1/2 lb chorizo sausage, cooked
- 2 large eggs, scrambled
- 1/4 cup shredded cheddar cheese
- 1/4 cup salsa
- Fresh cilantro for garnish

Instructions

1. Cook the chorizo in a skillet over medium heat until browned and cooked through.
2. Scramble the eggs in a separate skillet.
3. Warm the tortillas in a dry skillet or microwave.
4. Fill each tortilla with scrambled eggs and chorizo.
5. Top with shredded cheese, salsa, and cilantro.
6. Serve immediately.

Bacon, Egg, and Cheese Muffins

Ingredients

- 4 English muffins, split
- 4 slices bacon, cooked
- 4 large eggs
- 1/4 cup shredded cheddar cheese
- Salt and pepper to taste

Instructions

1. Toast the English muffins and cook the bacon until crispy.
2. In a skillet, fry the eggs to your desired doneness.
3. Assemble the muffins by layering bacon, eggs, and cheese on the bottom half of each muffin.
4. Place the top half of the muffin and serve warm.

Blueberry Muffins with Streusel Topping

Ingredients

- 1 1/2 cups all-purpose flour
- 3/4 cup sugar
- 2 tsp baking powder
- 1/2 tsp salt
- 1/2 cup milk
- 1/4 cup butter, melted
- 1 large egg
- 1 tsp vanilla extract
- 1 cup fresh or frozen blueberries

Streusel Topping:

- 1/4 cup flour
- 2 tbsp butter, cold and cubed
- 1/4 cup brown sugar
- 1/2 tsp cinnamon

Instructions

1. Preheat the oven to 350°F (175°C) and grease a muffin tin.
2. In a bowl, whisk together the flour, sugar, baking powder, and salt.
3. In another bowl, mix together the milk, melted butter, egg, and vanilla extract.
4. Combine the wet and dry ingredients, then gently fold in the blueberries.
5. For the streusel topping, mix flour, butter, brown sugar, and cinnamon in a bowl and rub together until crumbly.
6. Spoon the batter into muffin cups and sprinkle with streusel topping.
7. Bake for 18-20 minutes, or until a toothpick comes out clean. Let cool before serving.

Breakfast Sausage and Gravy

Ingredients

- 1/2 lb breakfast sausage
- 2 tbsp butter
- 2 tbsp all-purpose flour
- 2 cups milk
- Salt and pepper to taste
- 1/2 tsp cayenne pepper (optional)

Instructions

1. Cook the sausage in a skillet over medium heat until browned and crumbled.
2. Remove the sausage and set it aside. In the same skillet, melt the butter and stir in the flour to create a roux.
3. Slowly add the milk, whisking to avoid lumps.
4. Cook the gravy until thickened, about 5-7 minutes.
5. Stir in the sausage, season with salt, pepper, and cayenne pepper.
6. Serve the gravy over biscuits or toast.

Baked Avocado Eggs

Ingredients

- 2 ripe avocados
- 4 large eggs
- Salt and pepper to taste
- Fresh herbs for garnish (optional)

Instructions

1. Preheat the oven to 375°F (190°C).
2. Cut the avocados in half and remove the pits.
3. Scoop out a little bit of the flesh to create space for the eggs.
4. Place the avocado halves in a baking dish and crack an egg into each half.
5. Season with salt and pepper.
6. Bake for 12-15 minutes, or until the egg whites are set.
7. Garnish with fresh herbs and serve warm.

Vegan Pancakes with Maple Syrup

Ingredients

- 1 cup flour
- 1 tbsp sugar
- 2 tsp baking powder
- 1/2 tsp salt
- 1 cup almond milk (or any plant-based milk)
- 1 tbsp vegetable oil
- 1 tsp vanilla extract
- Maple syrup for serving

Instructions

1. In a bowl, whisk together the flour, sugar, baking powder, and salt.
2. Add the almond milk, vegetable oil, and vanilla extract, and mix until just combined.
3. Heat a non-stick skillet or griddle over medium heat and lightly grease.
4. Pour batter onto the skillet, cooking for 2-3 minutes on each side until golden brown.
5. Serve with maple syrup and enjoy!

Coconut Yogurt Parfait with Granola

Ingredients

- 1 cup coconut yogurt
- 1/4 cup granola
- 1/4 cup fresh berries (such as strawberries, blueberries, or raspberries)
- 1 tbsp honey (optional)
- A sprinkle of chia seeds (optional)

Instructions

1. In a glass or bowl, layer coconut yogurt at the bottom.
2. Top with granola, followed by fresh berries.
3. Drizzle with honey for extra sweetness, if desired.
4. Finish with a sprinkle of chia seeds for added texture.
5. Serve immediately or refrigerate for a quick grab-and-go breakfast.

Egg and Cheese Breakfast Croissant

Ingredients

- 1 buttery croissant, sliced in half
- 2 large eggs
- 1 slice cheddar cheese
- 1 tbsp butter
- Salt and pepper to taste

Instructions

1. Heat a non-stick skillet over medium heat and melt the butter.
2. Crack the eggs into the skillet, cooking them sunny-side up or scrambled, depending on your preference.
3. Place the croissant halves in the skillet to lightly toast them.
4. Once the eggs are done, place one on each croissant half and top with a slice of cheddar cheese.
5. Close the croissant and serve immediately for a delicious, cheesy breakfast sandwich.

Chocolate Chip Pancakes

Ingredients

- 1 cup all-purpose flour
- 2 tbsp sugar
- 2 tsp baking powder
- 1/2 tsp salt
- 1 cup milk
- 1 large egg
- 1/2 tsp vanilla extract
- 1/2 cup chocolate chips
- Butter for cooking

Instructions

1. In a bowl, whisk together flour, sugar, baking powder, and salt.
2. In another bowl, mix the milk, egg, and vanilla extract.
3. Add the wet ingredients to the dry ingredients and stir until combined, being careful not to overmix.
4. Gently fold in the chocolate chips.
5. Heat a griddle or skillet over medium heat and lightly grease with butter.
6. Pour batter onto the griddle, cooking until bubbles form on the surface. Flip and cook until golden brown.
7. Serve warm with maple syrup and extra chocolate chips if desired.

Smoothie with Spinach and Pineapple

Ingredients

- 1 cup fresh spinach
- 1 cup frozen pineapple chunks
- 1/2 banana
- 1/2 cup coconut water or almond milk
- 1 tbsp chia seeds (optional)
- Ice cubes (optional)

Instructions

1. Add spinach, pineapple, banana, and coconut water (or almond milk) into a blender.
2. Blend until smooth, adding ice cubes for extra chill or more liquid if needed.
3. Pour into a glass and sprinkle with chia seeds for added fiber and texture.
4. Serve immediately for a refreshing and nutrient-packed breakfast.

Baked Apple Cinnamon Oatmeal

Ingredients

- 1 1/2 cups rolled oats
- 1 1/2 cups almond milk
- 1 apple, peeled and diced
- 1 tsp cinnamon
- 1/2 tsp vanilla extract
- 2 tbsp maple syrup
- 1/4 cup chopped nuts (optional)

Instructions

1. Preheat your oven to 350°F (175°C) and grease a baking dish.
2. In a bowl, combine oats, almond milk, diced apple, cinnamon, vanilla extract, and maple syrup.
3. Pour the mixture into the greased baking dish and stir to combine.
4. Bake for 30-35 minutes, or until the oats are soft and the liquid is absorbed.
5. Top with chopped nuts for crunch, if desired, and serve warm.

Churro Waffles

Ingredients

- 1 cup waffle mix (or use homemade waffle batter)
- 1 tbsp cinnamon
- 1/4 cup sugar
- 1/2 cup butter, melted
- Maple syrup for serving

Instructions

1. Prepare the waffle batter according to the package instructions or your recipe.
2. In a small bowl, combine cinnamon and sugar.
3. Cook waffles in a preheated waffle iron.
4. While the waffles are still warm, brush them with melted butter and sprinkle with the cinnamon-sugar mixture.
5. Serve with maple syrup and enjoy a churro-inspired breakfast treat.

Grilled Cheese and Tomato Soup Breakfast

Ingredients

- 2 slices bread
- 2 slices cheddar cheese
- 1 tbsp butter
- 1 can tomato soup (or homemade)
- Fresh basil for garnish (optional)

Instructions

1. Heat the soup in a saucepan over medium heat, stirring occasionally.
2. Butter one side of each slice of bread. Place the cheese between the unbuttered sides of the bread to make a sandwich.
3. Grill the sandwich in a skillet over medium heat until both sides are golden brown and the cheese is melted.
4. Serve the grilled cheese alongside the warm tomato soup, garnished with fresh basil if desired.

Breakfast Pizza with Eggs and Bacon

Ingredients

- 1 pizza dough (store-bought or homemade)
- 2 large eggs
- 4 slices cooked bacon, crumbled
- 1/2 cup shredded mozzarella cheese
- 1 tbsp olive oil
- Fresh parsley for garnish

Instructions

1. Preheat your oven according to the pizza dough instructions.
2. Roll out the pizza dough onto a baking sheet and brush with olive oil.
3. Sprinkle mozzarella cheese evenly over the dough.
4. Crack the eggs onto the pizza, spacing them evenly.
5. Scatter the crumbled bacon on top.
6. Bake in the oven until the crust is golden and the eggs are cooked to your desired level (about 10-15 minutes).
7. Garnish with fresh parsley and serve immediately for a savory, breakfast-style pizza.

Apple Cinnamon French Toast Bake

Ingredients

- 4 cups cubed day-old bread
- 2 apples, peeled and diced
- 1 tsp cinnamon
- 1/2 cup milk
- 1/2 cup heavy cream
- 4 large eggs
- 1/4 cup maple syrup
- 1/2 tsp vanilla extract
- Pinch of salt
- Powdered sugar for garnish

Instructions

1. Preheat your oven to 350°F (175°C) and grease a 9x13-inch baking dish.
2. Layer the cubed bread in the baking dish, then top with the diced apples and sprinkle with cinnamon.
3. In a bowl, whisk together the milk, heavy cream, eggs, maple syrup, vanilla, and a pinch of salt.
4. Pour the egg mixture over the bread and apples, pressing the bread down to soak in the liquid.
5. Bake for 35-40 minutes, or until the top is golden and the center is set.
6. Dust with powdered sugar and serve warm for a cozy breakfast treat.

Chia Seed and Almond Pudding

Ingredients

- 1/4 cup chia seeds
- 1 cup almond milk
- 1 tbsp maple syrup
- 1/2 tsp vanilla extract
- Sliced almonds and fresh berries for topping

Instructions

1. In a bowl, combine chia seeds, almond milk, maple syrup, and vanilla extract.
2. Stir well to ensure the chia seeds are evenly mixed with the liquid.
3. Cover and refrigerate for at least 4 hours or overnight to allow the chia seeds to absorb the liquid and thicken.
4. Before serving, stir the pudding again and top with sliced almonds and fresh berries for added crunch and flavor.

Greek Yogurt with Honey and Almonds

Ingredients

- 1 cup Greek yogurt
- 1 tbsp honey
- 2 tbsp sliced almonds
- Fresh fruit (optional)

Instructions

1. Spoon the Greek yogurt into a bowl.
2. Drizzle with honey and sprinkle with sliced almonds.
3. Top with fresh fruit if desired, and serve immediately for a simple, healthy breakfast or snack.

Smoked Salmon and Cream Cheese Bagel

Ingredients

- 1 bagel, split and toasted
- 2 tbsp cream cheese
- 2-3 oz smoked salmon
- 1 tsp capers (optional)
- Fresh dill for garnish

Instructions

1. Spread cream cheese evenly over the toasted bagel halves.
2. Layer with smoked salmon and top with capers for a salty touch.
3. Garnish with fresh dill for an added pop of flavor.
4. Serve immediately as a savory, satisfying breakfast or brunch option.

Potato and Cheese Breakfast Skillet

Ingredients

- 2 medium potatoes, diced
- 1/2 cup shredded cheddar cheese
- 2 tbsp olive oil
- 1/4 cup diced onion
- 1/4 cup bell pepper, diced
- 2 eggs
- Salt and pepper to taste

Instructions

1. Heat olive oil in a skillet over medium heat.
2. Add diced potatoes and cook until golden and crispy, about 10-12 minutes.
3. Add diced onion and bell pepper, and cook until softened, about 5 minutes.
4. Season with salt and pepper, then make two wells in the mixture.
5. Crack an egg into each well and cook until the whites are set but the yolks are still runny.
6. Sprinkle with shredded cheddar cheese and let it melt.
7. Serve immediately, garnished with fresh herbs if desired.

Overnight Oats with Fruit and Nuts

Ingredients

- 1/2 cup rolled oats
- 1/2 cup almond milk (or any milk of choice)
- 1 tbsp chia seeds
- 1 tbsp honey or maple syrup
- 1/4 cup mixed berries
- 2 tbsp chopped nuts (e.g., almonds, walnuts, or pecans)

Instructions

1. In a jar or bowl, combine oats, almond milk, chia seeds, and honey.
2. Stir well, then cover and refrigerate overnight.
3. In the morning, top with fresh berries and chopped nuts.
4. Enjoy this easy, nutritious breakfast to start your day.

Cinnamon Sugar Donuts

Ingredients

- 1 1/2 cups all-purpose flour
- 1/2 cup sugar
- 1 tsp baking powder
- 1/2 tsp cinnamon
- 1/4 tsp salt
- 1/2 cup milk
- 2 large eggs
- 1/4 cup melted butter
- 1/2 tsp vanilla extract
- 1/4 cup sugar
- 1 tsp cinnamon (for coating)

Instructions

1. Preheat the oven to 350°F (175°C) and grease a donut pan.
2. In a bowl, combine flour, sugar, baking powder, cinnamon, and salt.
3. In another bowl, whisk together milk, eggs, melted butter, and vanilla extract.
4. Pour the wet ingredients into the dry ingredients and stir until just combined.
5. Spoon the batter into the donut pan, filling each cavity about 2/3 full.
6. Bake for 12-15 minutes or until golden and a toothpick comes out clean.
7. While the donuts cool slightly, mix the cinnamon and sugar for the coating.
8. Roll the warm donuts in the cinnamon sugar mixture and serve.

Maple Pecan Pancakes

Ingredients

- 1 1/2 cups all-purpose flour
- 2 tbsp sugar
- 2 tsp baking powder
- 1/2 tsp salt
- 1 cup milk
- 1 large egg
- 2 tbsp melted butter
- 1/2 cup chopped pecans
- Maple syrup for serving

Instructions

1. In a bowl, combine flour, sugar, baking powder, and salt.
2. In another bowl, whisk together milk, egg, and melted butter.
3. Pour the wet ingredients into the dry ingredients and stir until just combined.
4. Fold in chopped pecans.
5. Heat a skillet or griddle over medium heat and lightly grease with butter.
6. Pour the batter onto the skillet, cooking each pancake until bubbles form on the surface.
7. Flip and cook until golden brown on both sides.
8. Serve warm with maple syrup for a nutty, sweet breakfast delight.

Eggs in a Hole with Toast

Ingredients

- 2 slices of bread
- 2 large eggs
- 1 tbsp butter
- Salt and pepper to taste
- Fresh herbs for garnish (optional)

Instructions

1. Using a glass or cookie cutter, cut a hole in the center of each slice of bread.
2. Heat butter in a skillet over medium heat.
3. Place the bread slices in the skillet and crack an egg into the hole of each slice.
4. Cook for 2-3 minutes or until the egg whites are set. Flip and cook for another 1-2 minutes for a runny yolk, or longer for well-done eggs.
5. Season with salt and pepper and garnish with fresh herbs, if desired.
6. Serve warm for a delicious and simple breakfast.

Oatmeal with Brown Sugar and Raisins

Ingredients

- 1 cup rolled oats
- 2 cups water or milk
- 1/4 cup brown sugar
- 1/4 cup raisins
- A pinch of salt
- Ground cinnamon (optional)

Instructions

1. In a pot, bring water or milk to a boil.
2. Stir in the oats and reduce the heat to a simmer.
3. Cook for about 5 minutes, stirring occasionally, until the oats are soft and the liquid is absorbed.
4. Stir in brown sugar, raisins, and a pinch of salt.
5. Top with a sprinkle of cinnamon if desired.
6. Serve warm for a comforting, hearty breakfast.

Scrambled Eggs with Salsa and Sour Cream

Ingredients

- 4 large eggs
- 2 tbsp butter
- Salt and pepper to taste
- 2 tbsp salsa
- 2 tbsp sour cream
- Fresh cilantro for garnish (optional)

Instructions

1. Crack the eggs into a bowl and whisk them with salt and pepper.
2. Heat butter in a skillet over medium-low heat.
3. Pour the eggs into the skillet and gently stir with a spatula as they begin to set, making soft folds.
4. Once the eggs are scrambled and cooked through but still soft, remove from heat.
5. Top with salsa and a dollop of sour cream.
6. Garnish with fresh cilantro, if desired, and serve immediately.

Ricotta Pancakes with Lemon Zest

Ingredients

- 1 cup ricotta cheese
- 1 cup all-purpose flour
- 2 tbsp sugar
- 1 tsp baking powder
- 1/2 tsp baking soda
- 1/2 tsp salt
- 2 large eggs
- 1/2 cup milk
- 1 tsp vanilla extract
- Zest of 1 lemon
- Butter for cooking
- Maple syrup for serving

Instructions

1. In a bowl, combine ricotta, eggs, milk, vanilla extract, and lemon zest.
2. In a separate bowl, whisk together flour, sugar, baking powder, baking soda, and salt.
3. Add the dry ingredients to the wet ingredients and stir until just combined (the batter should be slightly lumpy).
4. Heat a griddle or non-stick skillet over medium heat and melt a small amount of butter.
5. Pour batter onto the skillet, using about 1/4 cup for each pancake.
6. Cook for 2-3 minutes per side or until golden brown and cooked through.
7. Serve warm with maple syrup for a sweet, citrusy twist on a breakfast favorite.

Spinach and Mushroom Frittata

Ingredients

- 6 large eggs
- 1 tbsp olive oil
- 1/2 cup mushrooms, sliced
- 1 cup fresh spinach, chopped
- 1/4 cup grated Parmesan cheese
- Salt and pepper to taste
- Fresh herbs for garnish (optional)

Instructions

1. Preheat the oven to 375°F (190°C).
2. In a bowl, whisk together eggs, salt, and pepper.
3. Heat olive oil in a skillet over medium heat. Add the sliced mushrooms and cook for 5-7 minutes until softened.
4. Add the spinach and cook for another 1-2 minutes until wilted.
5. Pour the beaten eggs over the mushrooms and spinach, ensuring even distribution.
6. Sprinkle Parmesan cheese on top.
7. Transfer the skillet to the oven and bake for 10-15 minutes, or until the frittata is set and golden on top.
8. Garnish with fresh herbs, if desired, and serve warm.

Breakfast Quesadilla with Sausage

Ingredients

- 2 flour tortillas
- 2 large eggs
- 1/2 cup cooked sausage, crumbled
- 1/4 cup shredded cheese (cheddar or your preference)
- 1/4 cup diced bell peppers (optional)
- 1/4 cup diced onions (optional)
- 1 tbsp butter or oil for cooking
- Salsa and sour cream for serving

Instructions

1. Scramble the eggs in a bowl and cook them in a skillet over medium heat with a little butter or oil until soft and just set.
2. In a separate skillet, cook the sausage until browned and fully cooked.
3. Place one tortilla in a large skillet over medium heat.
4. Sprinkle half of the cheese on the tortilla, then add the scrambled eggs, sausage, and optional vegetables.
5. Top with the remaining cheese and place the second tortilla on top.
6. Cook for 2-3 minutes, flipping halfway through, until the quesadilla is golden brown and the cheese is melted.
7. Slice into wedges and serve with salsa and sour cream on the side.

Sausage Patties with Biscuit Gravy

Ingredients

- 1 lb breakfast sausage
- 2 cups milk
- 2 tbsp butter
- 2 tbsp all-purpose flour
- Salt and pepper to taste
- 4-6 biscuits (store-bought or homemade)

Instructions

1. Shape the sausage into patties and cook them in a skillet over medium heat until browned and cooked through, about 4-5 minutes per side.
2. Remove the sausage from the skillet and set aside.
3. For the gravy, melt butter in the same skillet over medium heat, then whisk in the flour.
4. Slowly add milk while continuing to whisk, cooking until the gravy thickens (about 3-5 minutes).
5. Season with salt and pepper to taste.
6. Split the biscuits and spoon the gravy over them, topping with the sausage patties.
7. Serve warm for a hearty breakfast.

Warm Cinnamon Rolls with Cream Cheese Frosting

Ingredients

- 1 package refrigerated cinnamon roll dough (or homemade dough)
- 2 tbsp butter, melted
- 1 cup powdered sugar
- 4 oz cream cheese, softened
- 1/2 tsp vanilla extract
- Pinch of salt

Instructions

1. Preheat the oven and bake the cinnamon rolls according to the package instructions.
2. While the rolls are baking, mix the softened cream cheese, powdered sugar, vanilla extract, and a pinch of salt in a bowl until smooth.
3. Once the cinnamon rolls are baked and warm, drizzle the cream cheese frosting over the top.
4. Serve immediately for a sweet and indulgent breakfast treat.

Egg and Veggie Breakfast Wrap

Ingredients

- 2 large eggs
- 1/4 cup milk
- 1/2 cup mixed vegetables (spinach, bell peppers, onions, tomatoes)
- 1/4 cup shredded cheese (optional)
- 1 whole wheat tortilla
- 1 tbsp olive oil or butter for cooking
- Salt and pepper to taste

Instructions

1. Whisk the eggs and milk together in a bowl.
2. Heat the olive oil or butter in a skillet over medium heat and sauté the vegetables until soft, about 5 minutes.
3. Pour the egg mixture over the vegetables and cook until the eggs are scrambled and set.
4. Remove from heat and season with salt and pepper.
5. Lay the egg mixture in the center of the tortilla, sprinkle with cheese, and fold the sides of the tortilla to form a wrap.
6. Serve warm as a quick and nutritious breakfast.

Coconut Banana Smoothie

Ingredients

- 1 ripe banana
- 1/2 cup coconut milk (or almond milk)
- 1/2 cup Greek yogurt
- 1 tbsp honey or maple syrup (optional)
- 1/2 tsp vanilla extract
- Ice cubes (optional)

Instructions

1. Place the banana, coconut milk, Greek yogurt, honey, and vanilla extract in a blender.
2. Blend until smooth and creamy, adding ice cubes if you prefer a thicker consistency.
3. Pour into a glass and serve immediately for a tropical and refreshing breakfast smoothie.

Printed in the USA
CPSIA information can be obtained
at www.ICGtesting.com
CBHW081830191124
17645CB00018B/138

9 798330 543922